REX Collections
The Who

Edited by
MARCUS HEARN

Designed by
JAMES KING

Reynolds & Hearn Ltd
London

For Dave,
dreaming of a book about the 'Orrible 'Oo

Frontispiece: Marc Sharratt
Title page: Barry Peake

First published in 2005 by
Reynolds & Hearn Ltd
61a Priory Road
Kew Gardens
Richmond
Surrey TW9 3DH

Images © Rex Features 2005
Text © Marcus Hearn 2005

A CIP catalogue record for this book is available from the British Library.

ISBN 1 905287 06 2

Printed and bound in Great Britain by Biddles Ltd, King's Lynn, Norfolk.

Pete Townshend and Andy Summers of the Police in 1983.
Photograph: Richard Young

INTRODUCTION

'There's no way anyone could call us a pretty band.
You couldn't have picked four more ugly geezers!'
Roger Daltrey, 1975

Roger Daltrey, John Entwistle, Keith Moon and Pete
Townshend were hardly boy band material: abrasive,
arrogant and consumed by self-destructive urges, they
would not have flourished in the current climate of well
-groomed groups manufactured by reality TV shows.
Which is not to say that the Who weren't photogenic;
throughout the band's long and sometimes dramatic
career they gave picture editors plenty of inspiration.
The group's pioneering musical evolution throughout
the 1960s and early 1970s was matched by numerous
colourful images and breathtaking stagecraft.

Guitarist and principal songwriter Pete Townshend
became aware of the mod movement after reading an
article in the *Sunday Times Magazine* in spring 1964.
As a frustrated youngster, Townshend had thrown a
guitar amp at his grandmother. On stage at the Railway
Hotel in Harrow & Wealdstone in 1964 he accidentally
put his Rickenbacker through the ceiling and was
impressed by the reaction. Townshend indulged his
post-art college interest in pop-art with evocative results:
the Who became as notorious for their Union flag jackets
and shattered guitars as for their music.

The Who embraced psychedelia in 1967 before
Townshend reinvented the group – and indeed popular

music – with his audacious 'rock opera' *Tommy*.
Townshend's 'deaf, dumb and blind kid' subsequently
became the subject of a successful film and
Broadway musical.

Townshend's restless creativity was the heart of the
group, but Daltrey, Entwistle and Moon were also superb
musicians who provided a formidable engine for his
ideas. The conflict between the different personalities in
the Who threatened to tear them apart in the early days,
but it also helped to generate a fruitful energy on stage
and in the studio.

The group began the 1970s with a trio of classic
albums, each a progression of their sound and each a
critical and commercial success. From *Live At Leeds*
(1970) through their masterpiece *Who's Next* (1971) to
arguably their last great album, *Quadrophenia* (1973),
the Who's trajectory was bold and groundbreaking.
It couldn't last. Amid concerns about damage to his
hearing, Townshend struggled to tailor his ideas to
the group's thundering presentation. Progress and
productivity faltered, and in 1978 Keith Moon died
as an indirect result of his chronic alcoholism.

In a statement issued after Moon's death, Townshend
wrote: 'We have lost our great comedian, our supreme
melodramatist, the man, who apart from being the
most unpredictable and spontaneous drummer in rock,
would have set himself alight if he thought it would make
the audience laugh or jump out of its seats.' The Who
continued with a new drummer, Kenney Jones, but the
in-fighting continued and Townshend was so ashamed

The Who live at Madison Square Garden,
New York, Saturday 22 May 2004.
Photograph: Albert Ferreira

of the new material that he split the band in 1982.

The Who has endured through sporadic reunions, surviving the departure of Jones and the death of Entwistle. There have only been a handful of (admittedly impressive) new songs since 1982, Daltrey and Townshend seemingly content to celebrate their legacy with typically ear-bleeding volume. 'We owe it to our fans, our original fans that are our age now, to show them how to live,' said Daltrey in 2004. 'And you don't fucking give up because one of your mates died. You carry on.'

***

Compiling a collection of Who photographs from the vast archive of Rex Features presented some ultimately rewarding challenges. As a London-based agency, it was perhaps unsurprising to discover that a number of the group's most significant North American jaunts (Monterey, Woodstock, the farewell tour) were relatively under-represented. The compensations, however, were astonishing. Chief among them were the colourful pictures taken by Hungarian photographer Dezo Hoffman. A familiar figure on the music scene throughout the 1960s, Hoffman was a craftsman trusted by such disparate personalities as Dusty Springfield and Jimi Hendrix. Hoffman took hundreds of stills on the set of ITV's *Ready, Steady, Go!*, creating intimate and dramatic compositions for contemporary teen magazines. His pictures of the Who's appearances on *RSG!* and the BBC's *A Whole Scene Going* are among the highlights here.

Also worthy of mention is David Magnus, whose Covent Garden studio session captured the Who on the cusp of their commercial breakthrough. Piecing together his 'Photo Love' sequence featuring John Entwistle and Carole-Anne Martin was the most frustrating and intriguing part of the research for this book. This is one of a number of sequences of pictures that have been reconstructed for possibly the first time since they left the photographers' dark rooms.

Hugh Vanes bravely accompanied the boys in the back of their van during a UK tour in April 1966. His candid pictures are a valuable record of a time when having a Top Ten hit didn't absolve you from fetching spare tyres and living out of greasy spoon cafés. In 1966 Harry Goodwin brought a traditional portrait approach to some scruffy subjects and in 1969 Peter Saunders caught the snarling, animalistic Who in full flight. John Selby, David Thorpe and Richard Young depicted the majesty of 'The Greatest Rock And Roll Band In The World' in the mid- to late-1970s, while Nils Jorgensen, Dave Hogan and Brian Rasic chart the rocky path of the reunion-era Who with a crisp and unforgiving scrutiny.

There are many other outstanding photographers represented here. The criteria for inclusion accommodated such considerations as artistic and technical quality over the desire to present a comprehensive retrospective of the Who's career. And there are no apologies for giving disproportionate space to pictures from the group's 1960s and 70s heyday.

Sincere thanks to the librarians and other staff at Rex Features, and especially to New Business Manager Glen Marks, whose initiative and encouragement helped make the *Rex Collections* series of books possible. Thanks are also due to Andrew Godfrey for additional scanning and image restoration.

It's been *smashing*…

Pages 8-11 →
Bass guitarist John Entwistle (page 8), drummer Keith Moon (page 9), lead singer Roger Daltrey (page 10) and guitarist Pete Townshend (page 11) photographed in early July 1964. The young mods had just released their first single, 'I'm The Face' B/W 'Zoot Suit', under the name the High Numbers.

The group had begun to take shape at Acton County Grammar School For Boys in 1961. Daltrey was in a band with Entwistle and asked Townshend to join them. Townshend took some persuading, but has fond memories of 'Three snotty-nosed school kids with mashed potato on our lapels!'

Keith Moon joined in spring 1964 and the classic line-up was complete. Roger Daltrey: 'We got Keith, this kid we didn't know out of the audience, on the drums and it was like this fucking jet engine starting. I was like, "What the fuck's THIS?" Really, we couldn't have had any other drummer. He was incredible.'

Photographs: Dezo Hoffman

Pages 12-15

The group reverted to its previous name, the Who, at the end of 1964. By way of an announcement, Daltrey, Entwistle, Moon and Townshend posed for pictures in Covent Garden (the crate in the latter pictures came from the nearby fruit and vegetable market). A note on the back of one of the original prints reveals that the pictures were also to be used to publicise the Who's first single, 'I Can't Explain', which was due to be released in January 1965.

'We were all trying to outdo each other by looking pretty,' says Daltrey, recalling the session. 'I'm wearing the famed zoot suit, which came from our publicist Peter Meaden.'

Photographs: David Magnus

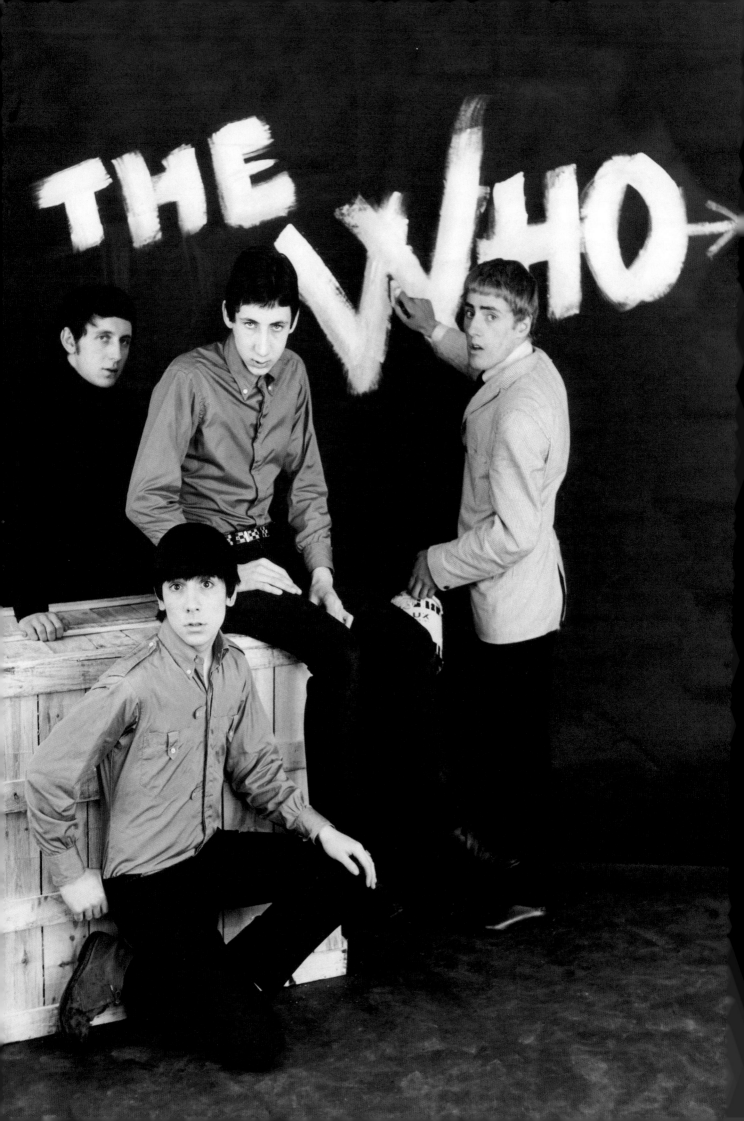

Playing the Blueopera R&B
Club in Edmonton, London,
on Thursday 25 March 1965.
The previous day the group
had recorded their second
appearance on the BBC's
Top of the Pops to promote
'I Can't Explain'.

Photograph: Dezo Hoffman

The Who made a huge impact on Associated-Rediffusion's *Ready, Steady, Go!* Produced at Television House in London, *Ready, Steady, Go!* was transmitted by ITV on Friday evenings from August 1963 to December 1966.

'The atmosphere in that studio was terrific,' recalls the show's assistant editor, Vicki Wickham. 'Right from the start we attracted the best looking mods with great haircuts, great gear and great attitude.'

Sadly, only two of the group's performances from the programme still exist.

Photograph: Dezo Hoffman

Pages 20-25
These pictures were taken during camera rehearsals for *Ready, Steady, Go!* on Friday 6 August 1965. Shortly after these shots were taken Roger Daltrey was taken ill; the remaining members of the band performed as a three-piece when the show was broadcast live that evening.

Photographs: Dezo Hoffman

Pages 26-29

Daltrey had recovered in time to rejoin the band later on 6 August, as they performed at the 5th National Jazz & Blues Festival at Richmond, Surrey. The typically vigorous show was filmed by an American television crew; clips appear in the documentary film *The Kids Are Alright* and the subsequent compilation *30 Years of Maximum R&B Live*.

Photographs: Dezo Hoffman

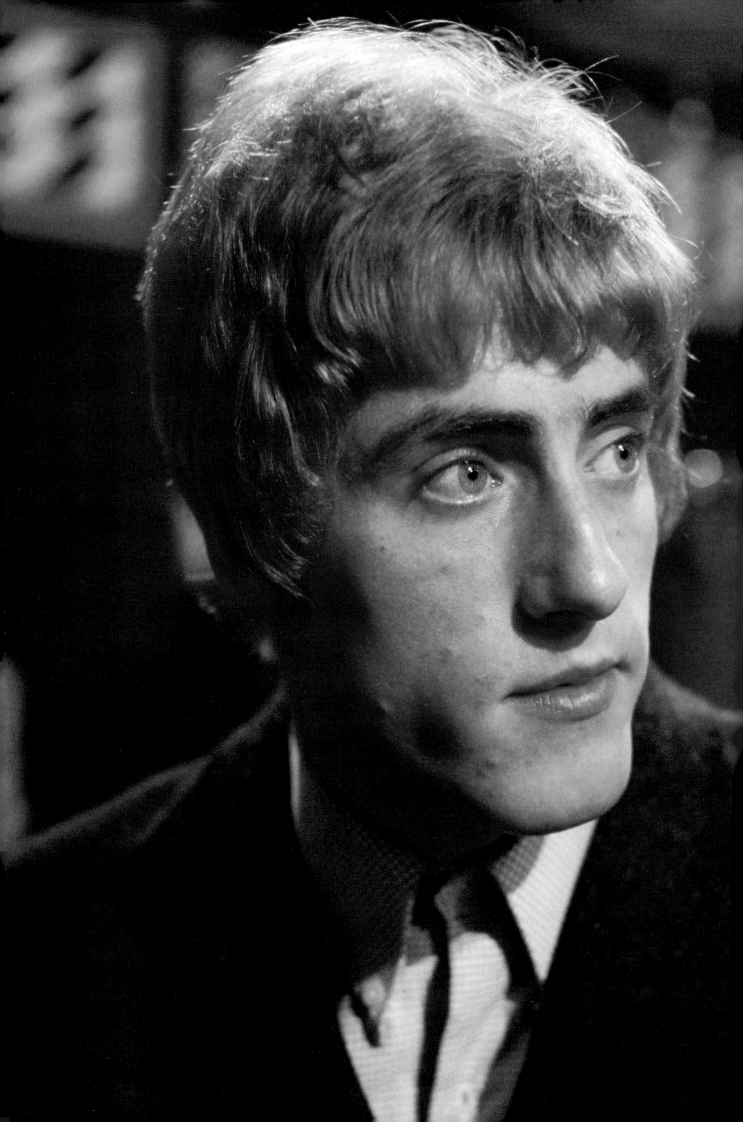

Pages 30-33

Portraits of Daltrey and Townshend taken during camera rehearsals for *Ready, Steady, Go!* on Friday 3 December 1965. Keith Moon's absence from this session could be explained by the fact that he arrived at Television House two hours late. He came up with some feeble excuses when interviewed by *NME* journalist Keith Altham later that afternoon: 'It was warm in bed. No, that's wrong – I'm ill.'

Moon told Altham that rumours of feuding within the group were true: 'I don't like half our records and Roger is the reason. He likes all this soul material and far out stuff... I like the Everly Brothers and Dion sounds... Roger and I disagree on a number of things.'

Photographs: Dezo Hoffman, Marc Sharratt

Pages 34-49
Pre-recording the Christmas Eve edition of *Ready, Steady, Go!*
on Friday 17 December 1965. For the final picture in this session
Townshend and Moon are joined by the programme's co-host
Cathy McGowan, fresh from her starring role in *Cinderella*,
the show's mini-pantomime.

Photographs: Dezo Hoffman, Kay Cooper (pages 35, 36, 42)

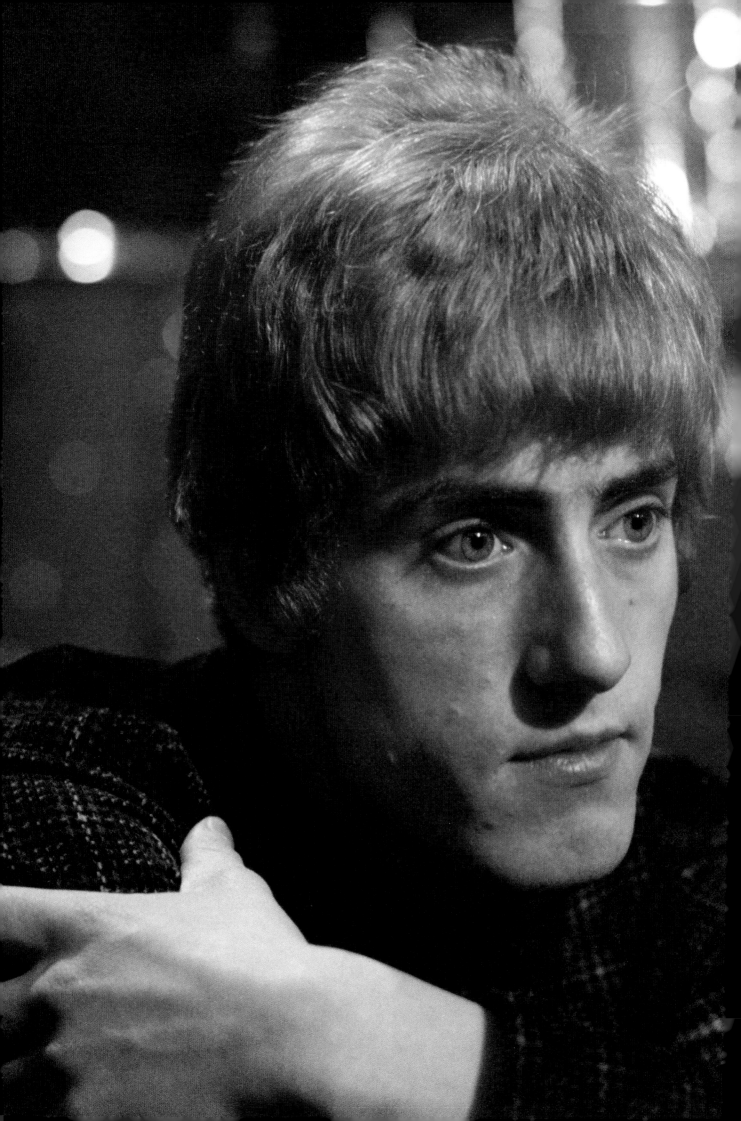

Pages 51-59

The group's appearance on the BBC's *A Whole Scene Going*
was recorded at Television Centre on Wednesday 5 January 1966.
Following a mimed performance in Studio 7, Townshend submitted
himself to a Q&A session with the show's earnest presenters.
Clips from this awkward exchange would prove a highlight of the
documentary film *The Kids Are Alright* 13 years later.

When asked why he didn't give the group some 'musical quality',
Townshend replied: 'If you steer clear of quality you're alright,
you know?'

Later in the interview he accused the Beatles of being
'flippin' lousy'.

Photographs: Dezo Hoffman

54

Portraits of the band from 1966. 'Off-stage, the group gets on terribly badly,' admitted Townshend in a promo film shot the previous year. 'The singer's a Shepherds Bush geezer who wants everything to be a big laugh and when it isn't he thinks something's going terribly wrong. The bass player doesn't seem to be terribly interested in anything. The drummer's a completely different person to anyone I've ever met.'

Photographs: Harry Goodwin

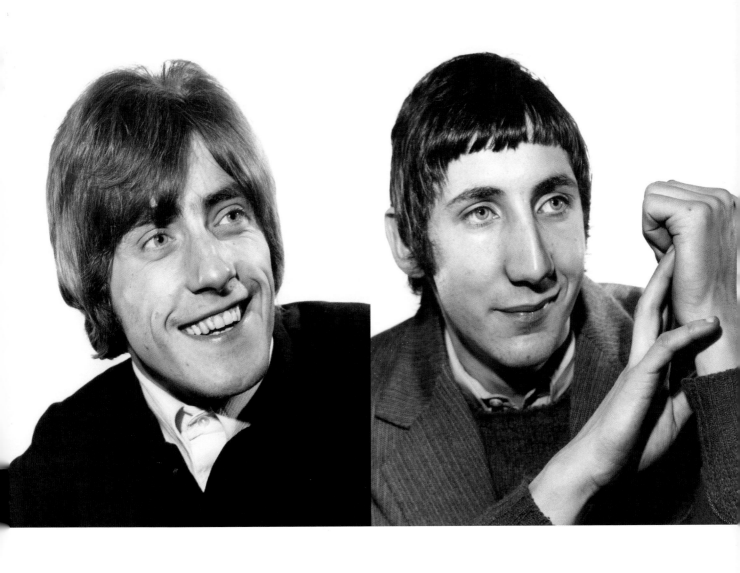

An effort at a light-hearted studio shot from 1966. The group had been mods since 1964, but Daltrey never felt entirely comfortable with the required look. 'I was always a rocker trying to compete in a mod's uniform,' he says. 'Not that I didn't like mod; I loved it. I just didn't suit it. I was very skinny back then, but I've got big shoulders, I've got a big chest, my shape just didn't suit it, so it was like trying to fit a pint into a half-pint pot.'

Daltrey struggled to tame his naturally curly hair ('to be a mod with curly hair was like having the pox') using a product called Dippety-Do. The mixed results earned him the band nickname 'Dip'.

Photograph: Dezo Hoffman

Pages 65-71

Friday 8 April 1966: 'Substitute' is in the charts and the Who continue their gruelling schedule of live performances by playing the Queen's Hall in Leeds.

The pictures on the next seven pages begin the morning after, with Townshend eating breakfast in his hotel. He is reading a *New Musical Express* report on the Who's recent appearance in a French edition of *Ready, Steady, Go!* Entwistle settles for yoghurt in a less salubrious café; Moon for a drink and a cigarette.

A picture taken from the van shows Townshend fetching a replacement tyre for the journey out of Leeds. The final shot in the session has Townshend supervising backstage preparations for that evening's gig in Buxton.

Photographs: Hugh Vanes

Pages 72-79

A *Ready, Steady, Go!* session from Tuesday 18 October 1966, during camera rehearsals for a 16-minute extravaganza that was recorded later that day. The group's eclectic repertoire included 'Batman', 'Cobwebs And Strange' and 'Rule Britannia'. The programme was broadcast on Friday 21 October.

The Who recorded their final *RSG!* appearance on Tuesday 20 December. 'I liked the atmosphere – it's very free and easy,' Keith Moon told *Melody Maker* later that month. 'Special thanks to the woman in the canteen who gave us our tea free. I suppose they come and they go. It'll certainly leave a gap between 6.30 and 7.00pm on a Friday, but I won't be mourning.'

Photographs: David Redfern

Pages 81-89

Thursday 2 March 1967: An intriguing sequence of pictures that follows glamorous Who fan Carole-Anne Martin as she accompanies John Entwistle to the Marquee Club in London. Entwistle joins his fellow band members for a live performance that was recorded by the German television programme *Beat Club* (extracts appear in *The Kids Are Alright*, *Who's Better, Who's Best* and *30 Years of Maximum R&B Live*). As Carole-Anne watches the group Rex photographers are taking pictures from both sides of the stage.

  With the gig over, Carole-Anne waves goodbye to her idol at the end of the afternoon.

Photographs: David Magnus, Ray Stevenson (page 88)

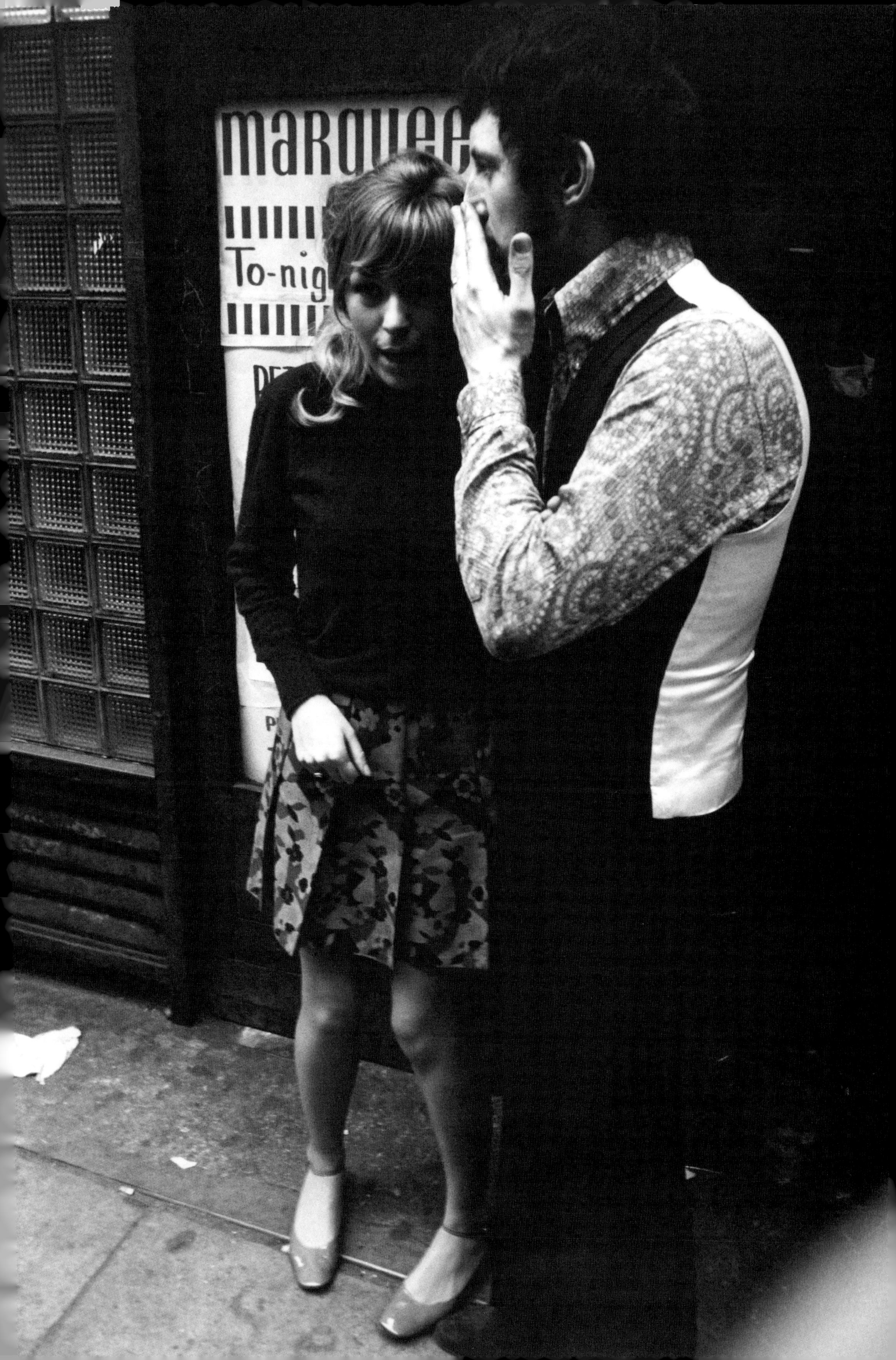
marquee
To-nig

Pages 90-93 →

The Who toured Germany for two weeks in April 1967. Dezo Hoffman went with them, taking colour pictures of the group in the Black Forest and, on Thursday 13 April, the Löwenbräu brewery in Munich!

'I don't think I ever wore anything I wasn't totally happy with,' says Daltrey, reflecting on the fashions of 1967. 'I mean, I think it got preposterous after the mod period when the flower-power thing came in. Now that was preposterous, that was fucking ridiculous. But it was total bravado.'

Photographs: Dezo Hoffman

Pages 94-95 ➔

'Monterey wasn't any fun at *all*,' says Townshend, but the Who's appearance at the Californian festival on Sunday 18 June 1967 effectively launched the group in America. Fearful of being upstaged by the Jimi Hendrix Experience, the Who went on first and indulged in their usual stage violence. Experience drummer Mitch Mitchell would describe the Who as 'a bloody hard act to follow' but Hendrix refused to be outdone. At the end of the Experience set Hendrix set his guitar *on fire…*

Photographs: Bruce Fleming

Pages 96-105
The Who's scene-stealing performance at *The Rolling Stones' Rock and Roll Circus* was a contributory factor in the Stones' decision to shelve their proposed television special. In comparison with the Stones, the Who looked and sounded like a group at the peak of their powers. The complete programme would not be released until 1996.

These pictures, taken on Tuesday 10 December and Wednesday 11 December 1968, show the group limbering up and performing 'A Quick One, While He's Away' at the InterTel Studios in Wembley. Moon arrived at rehearsals in full clown make-up, then poured beer onto his snare drums for added effect.

'We came on and had one run-through and one take of our mini-opera and blew them away,' remembered Entwistle.

Photographs: David Magnus (pages 98-99, 101-105),
Mike Randolph (pages 96-97), David Thorpe (page 100)

Pages 106-107

Another light-hearted publicity shoot, this time from early 1969. Townshend's groundbreaking 'rock opera' *Tommy* – about the spiritual awakening and redemption of a deaf, dumb and blind pinball player – was about to effect the Who's transformation from a faltering singles act to an albums-based rock group.

Some people, however, would find the ambitious double album difficult to appreciate. Townshend recalls that Radio 1 DJ Tony Blackburn dismissed *Tommy* as 'sick' and claimed that the single 'Pinball Wizard' (released in March 1969) 'shouldn't be allowed' on the air.

Moon retaliated by throwing his drumsticks at Blackburn during an edition of *Top of the Pops*.

'I don't want him to feel intimidated by groups like us,' Townshend subsequently wrote in *Melody Maker*, 'but I don't want him to be under the impression that when he knocks our work, which he has a perfect right to do, we will not knock back.'

Photographs: Marc Sharratt

← Pages 108-109
The Who play the Albert Hall on Saturday 5 May 1969. 'Everyone in the band started to define their images a lot more,' says Townshend of changes that occurred at the end of the decade. 'I used to go on wearing a boiler suit and Dr Martens *in defiance* of fashion.'

Photographs: Peter Saunders

Pages 110-119

In contrast with Townshend's anti-fashion, Daltrey became ever more flamboyant, as seen in these pictures from the Who's performance at the Isle of Wight Festival on Saturday 30 August 1969. 'I was always into American native culture and a friend of mine was making buckskins so I had a suit made,' says Daltrey.

Daltrey's formidable stage act now extended to swinging his microphone high above his head and out towards the audience. It was a skill that had came in useful when angry teddy boys threw coins at the stage during the Albert Hall gig. 'One cut me above my right eye,' recalls Daltrey. 'The guy who did it was wedged up against the stage and by then I could swing the mic so accurately I could take a cigarette out of someone's mouth. I got him full in the face!'

Photographs: Brian McCreeth (pages 110-111, 114-115),
Peter Saunders (pages 116-119), Mike Randolph (pages 112-113)

Pages 120-121
Rehearsing and performing 'The Seeker' on *Top of the Pops*,
Thursday 26 March 1970. 'I hate singles,' said Entwistle in 1976.
'I hate the whole thing about *Top of the Pops*.'

Photographs: Harry Goodwin

Page 122
On stage at the Fête de L'Humanité in Paris on Saturday 9 September 1972.
Photograph: Jacques Bernard

Page 123
Moon as J.D. Clover in the 1972 film *That'll Be The Day*.
Photograph: Brian Moody

Page 124
Summer 1974: Daltrey stars as Tommy in the Ken Russell film of the same name. 'Ken has been great,' said Daltrey the following year. 'He trusts me so much, and I've never been trusted like that by anyone, not even the Who... I'm a very physical and emotional person and Ken has managed to get out of me what I really am.'

Page 125
Daltrey with his *Tommy* co-star Ann-Margret.

Pages 126-129

'I still think the Who's a fucking good band,' said Daltrey, prior to rehearsals for the long awaited tour of 1975. 'It's just that I feel we've seen better days. We'll put that right, though.'

These pictures were taken at the King's Hall in Manchester in early October. The recently released album, *The Who By Numbers*, may have betrayed a decline in the quality of the group's recorded output but the tour certainly lived up to its defiant title: 'The Greatest Rock And Roll Band In The World'.

Photographs: John Selby

Pages 130-135
The Who reconvened in 1977 to shoot concert footage for the forthcoming documentary film *The Kids Are Alright*. These pictures were taken during a rehearsal at the Gaumont State Cinema in Kilburn, London, on Wednesday 14 December. After over a year apart from each other the band was rusty and, more seriously, it soon became apparent that Keith Moon's alcoholism had taken a devastating effect on his talent as well as his personal life. The film's director, Jeff Stein, took the decision to largely abandon the footage from this private concert (filmed the day after, Thursday 15th) and stage another concert at Shepperton Studios in May the following year. This concert, footage from which features in the finished film, would prove to be Moon's final performance with the Who.

On Thursday 7 September 1978 Keith Moon accidentally overdosed on the prescribed sedative Chlormethiazole and died of a heart attack. He was 32 years old.

Photographs: David Thorpe

Pages 136-139

Record company obligations, and a genuine desire to expand the range and scope of the Who's music, dictated that the band should continue after Moon's death. Former Faces drummer Kenney Jones was recruited as a new equal partner and John 'Rabbit' Bundrick added keyboards. 'I liked [Jones] for his simplicity and directness and for the similarity of our backgrounds,' says Townshend. 'He came up at the same time and had a similar success. He was one of the few British drummers who could fill Keith's shoes.'

Jones made his debut with the Who at London's Rainbow Theatre on Wednesday 2 May 1979. These pictures were taken on Saturday 5 May in an amphitheatre in Fréjus, outside Nice. The Who were playing two concerts in the 10,000-seat venue (on 5 and 6 May) to promote the screenings of the films *Quadrophenia* and *The Kids Are Alright* at the Cannes Film Festival.

'It was instantly apparent that the Who had lost none of their power,' wrote Chris Welch in *Melody Maker* after watching the 5 May gig. 'They have, if anything, developed a new locomotive energy, much of it stemming from Jones' zealous accuracy and relentless drive.'

Photographs: Richard Young

Page 140
The Who joined the bill at the Concert For Kampuchea benefit gig at the Hammersmith Odeon on Friday 28 December 1979. Townshend in particular had fun, telling the audience at the end 'it was *most* enjoyable.'

Photograph: Richard Young

Page 141
Despite a Top Ten single, 'You Better You Bet', 1981 saw morale in the band sink to a new low. Already drinking heavily, Townshend succumbed to his insecurities about his ability to write for the band and, towards the end of the year, developed a heroin habit.

'I became so utterly disenchanted with the Who,' he says. 'They really were pathetic in their last days – a dire, shadowy, awful, money-making desolate dinosaur. Dinosaur is just too high a term. Just fucking awful.'

The band's final album, *It's Hard*, was released in September 1982 to largely negative reviews. The so-called farewell tour began the same month and ended on Friday 17 December at Maple Leaf Gardens in Toronto.

Photograph: Richard Young

→ Pages 142-143
The Who during their farewell tour of 1982. 'With a shit record out, with a *dead drummer*, we could still do it,' says Townshend.

Photographs: Sten M. Rosenlund

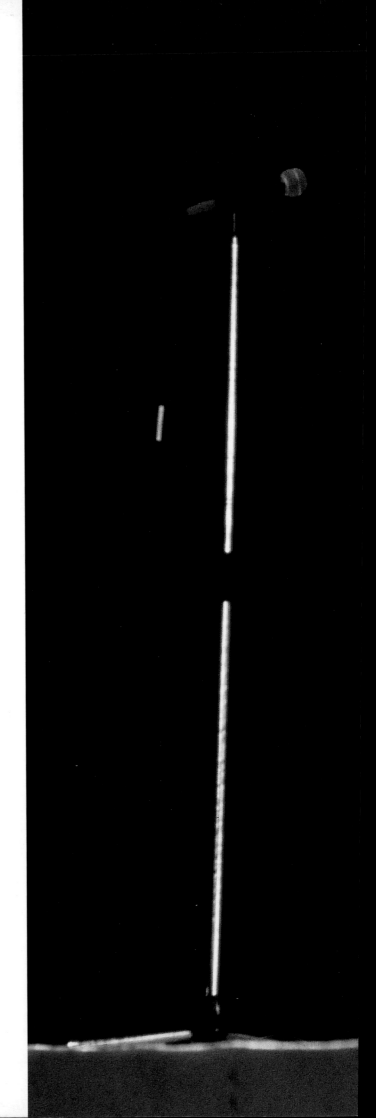

Pages 144-147
Wembley Stadium, Saturday 13 July 1985: Live Aid would not have been complete without a reunion of the now legendary Who. The event's co-organiser, Bob Geldof, later admitted that persuading Daltrey, Entwistle, Jones and Townshend had been like trying to get 'one man's four ex-wives together'. Despite a performance of 'Won't Get Fooled Again' that could charitably be described as under-rehearsed, the Who made a considerable impact with their brief but powerful set.

Photographs: John Rogers (pages 144-145),
Nils Jorgensen (page 146), Richard Young (page 147)

The three-man Who announce British tour dates in 1989, the band's 25th anniversary year. 'The decision to do it was not all disconnected from money,' said Townshend during rehearsals. Kenney Jones had grown impatient waiting for the band to reform, and there had reportedly been friction between him and Daltrey.

Photograph: Nils Jorgensen

Session drummer Simon Phillips joined the Who and numerous other musicians (including a brass section, backing singers, percussionist and second guitarist) during the band's 25th anniversary tour. This picture was taken at the Universal Amphitheatre in Los Angeles on Thursday 24 August, during an all-star charity performance of *Tommy*.

Photograph: André Csillag

Pages 149-151

Wembley Arena, October 1989. Hearing problems, largely caused
by 20 years of high volume headphone use, led Townshend to take
a cautious approach to the onstage sound levels during the 25th
anniversary tour. For a large part of each show he played acoustic
guitar in a 'quiet area' of the stage. 'I've been trying to reassure people
that there is genuine, explosive excitement in acoustic rhythm guitar,'
he said. 'I can make acoustic guitar *fly*.'

Photographs: Nils Jorgensen

Page 152

Possibly in an effort to remain consistent with his earlier assertion that the Who would never reform, Townshend described the 29 June 1996 performance of *Quadrophenia* in Hyde Park as a 'Who event' rather than a reunion. During rehearsals the day before, special guest Gary Glitter accidentally hit Daltrey in the face with a microphone stand. Daltrey covered his bruise with an eye patch.

Photograph: Richard Young

Page 153

Performing *Quadrophenia* at Earl's Court, Friday 6 December 1996.

Photograph: Brian Rasic

Pages 154-155

The Who returned to a more satisfying, stripped down stage presentation for subsequent reunions. Following an acclaimed five-month tour the band played a benefit for the Teenage Cancer Trust at the Albert Hall on Monday 27 November 2000. Accompanied by 'Rabbit' Bundrick on keyboards and Zak Starkey on drums, the revitalised Who delivered a mesmerising performance.

'If people want to hear me, I'll play,' said Entwistle, pictured above with a small video camera attached to his bass guitar during his performance of '5.15'. 'I don't care if it's fun or not. I can't do anything else… I want to live to be an eccentric old man.'

It was not to be. Entwistle died of a heart attack on Thursday 27 June 2002, shortly before a US tour was due to begin. The devastated Daltrey and Townshend had little option but to continue: they hastily recruited session bassist Pino Palladino and the tour belatedly began at the Hollywood Bowl in Los Angeles on Monday 1 July. Townshend announced from the stage: 'It's hard to think of a more appropriate place to kick this off – full of emptiness and deep rivers of shallow nothingness.'

Photographs: Dave Hogan

Page 156

Daltrey and Townshend lead the Who onstage at a Teenage Cancer Trust benefit held at the Albert Hall on Monday 29 March 2004.

Photograph: Richard Young

Page 157

Saturday 12 June 2004: The Who play the Isle of Wight Festival for the first time in 34 years.

Photograph: Brian Rasic

Pages 158-159 ➜

Twenty years after Live Aid, the Who deliver a considerably more polished performance of 'Won't Get Fooled Again' at the massive Live 8 event in Hyde Park on Saturday 2 July 2005.

'I don't know whether the notes are quite the same as they used to be, because I'm a lot older, but they're good enough,' says Daltrey. 'As long as that passion remains we'll go on doing it.'

Photographs: Brian Rasic

Photograph: Adrian Sherratt

REFERENCES

Articles
Altham, Keith. 'Who Admit They're Feuding'. *New Musical Express*, 10 December 1965
Anon. 'Pop Think In'. *Melody Maker*, 31 December 1966
Chapman, Rob. 'Keith Moon: Patent British Exploding Drummer'. *Mojo*, September 1998
Dellar, Fred. 'Ready, Steady, Go! begins'. *Mojo*, August 2005
Fortnam, Ian. 'Who Dares Wins'. *Classic Rock*, April 2004
Goddard, Simon. 'The Kids Are Alright'. *Uncut*, January 2003
Goddard, Simon. 'I'm Free'. *Uncut*, April 2004
Harris, John. 'Did loads of drugs, made loads of money, smashed loads of guitars'. *Q*, June 1996
Ingham, John. 'Is this the right man for Mayor of Acton?'. *Sounds*, 28 February 1976
Resnicoff, Matt. 'Godhead Revisited'. *Guitar Player*, September 1989
Shaar Murray, Charles. 'Conversations With Pete'. *New Musical Express*, April 1980
Simmonds, Chris. 'Who Exclusive!'. *Beat Instrumental*, July 1975
Snow, Mat. 'Any Old Iron'. *Sounds*, 1 July 1989
Sutcliffe, Phil. 'Life Thru A Lens'. *Q*, April 2002
Townshend, Pete. 'The Pete Townshend Page'. *Melody Maker*, 14 November 1970
Welch, Chris. 'Vive Le 'Oo!'. *Melody Maker*, 19 May 1979
Young, Charles M. 'Who's Back'. *Musician*, July 1989

Books
Black, Johnny. *Eyewitness: The Who*. London: Carlton, 2001
Fletcher, Tony. *Dear Boy: The Life of Keith Moon*. London: Omnibus, 1998
Marsh, Dave. *Before I Get Old*. London: Plexus, 1983
Mitchell, Mitch (and John Platt). *The Hendrix Experience*. London: Pyramid, 1990

Special mention should be made of *Anyway Anyhow Anywhere: The Complete Chronicle of the Who 1958-1978* by Andy Neill and Matt Kent (London: Virgin, 2002). This meticulous account proved especially useful in helping to identify certain pictures from the mid-1960s.